OTHER SIDE

How to overcome the Dark side of Loneliness

Peter Smultz

INTRODUCTION

If you've ever seen a picture of someone lonely, you probably think of someone older than 65 sitting alone, maybe in the dark, looking wistfully into the distance or longingly out a window. However, such images are false: Actually, young people are the ones who say they are lonely the most, and these images of being alone don't match what it's like to be alone in adolescence and early adulthood. Typically, those years are spent with people like: at home, at work, or school "The BBC's Loneliness Experiment, which polled 55,000 people from around the world, found that 40% of 16-24-year-olds reported experiencing loneliness frequently or very frequently".

A negative emotional response to a discrepancy between the relationships we have and those we desire can be defined as loneliness. This means that if we don't feel like others understand us or have interests in common with us, we might feel alone in their company. Loneliness can be a difficult experience, characterized by feelings of sadness, frustration, anger, and hopelessness. However, it can also help motivate us to reconnect with and reevaluate our relationships to strengthen (or seek out) the ones that mean the most to us. To determine what needs to be altered, we might pay closer attention to how our interactions with other people make us feel when we are alone. This mechanism is thought to be connected to our evolved need to be part of a group to avoid being alone and vulnerable.

Consider the following scenario, to which you might relate. Throughout high school, you maintain a close circle of friends, and some of those friends accompany you to college. You are initially pleased to have these high school buddies by your side. However, as you all settle in, your high school friends begin to form new friendships with people whose interests you don't share. You are left wondering where you fit in, and you realize that the closeness you had with your high school friends is missing: You begin to experience isolation. You might try to fit in with the new friend groups and find common ground as a way to deal with these feelings. Alternatively, you might decide that the old friendships no longer match who you are, so you look for new ones.

Most people don't feel lonely for long; It is brief and will go away when they reconnect. However, chronic loneliness can hurt a person's well-being for some people. The stigma associated with loneliness is one factor that contributes to people remaining in a state of constant isolation. Lonely people are frequently portrayed in negative ways: as introverts, narcissists, or socially awkward; consequently, individuals do not wish to be associated with loneliness. Because it is typically portrayed as being about social isolation—a lack of contact with other people—a person who is surrounded by others might not believe that they should qualify as lonely. They might think that their feelings of loneliness are wrong, which might cause them to self-judgment and make it hard for them to get help. However, research indicates that most people will experience loneliness at some point in their lives.

Loneliness can occur at any time in our lives; however, certain aspects of adolescence and young adulthood are more likely to cause it.

CHAPTER ONE

Common Experiences that Signify Loneliness

Talking about the provision of guides on humanity for self-development cannot be addressed without knowing the causes and I have carried out certain research that has brought me to a conclusion listed below:

Desire for friends

During adolescence and early adulthood, our friendships play a more and more significant role in providing us with emotional support. Young people, according to research, have higher expectations for their friendships than adults do; They exhibit a preference for greater frequency of contact with friends, greater intimacy, and companionship. It makes sense that feeling like we don't "fit in," which is something that so many young people experience, causes loneliness because loneliness helps us stay safe in our social world.

Our developing sense of self—discovering who we are—has an impact on our relationships during adolescence and early adulthood.

Identity shifts

That frequently entails altering one's aesthetics, values, and beliefs, as well as attempting new things.

When your friends are going through the same thing as you but don't want to go down the same path as you, it can be hard. You may discover that your values do not align with one another or that you do not feel accepted by your previous friends. You might be teased for not fitting in in some situations. That can be a problem, especially for people who are stigmatized because of their race, ethnicity, sexual orientation, gender, disability, or mental health issues. Keep in mind that many people don't feel like they've found their "crowd" until they're older or in their early twenties, but with time and experience come new opportunities to form such relationships.

Changes in life

like moving to a new school or university, can be difficult. Adjusting to a new environment takes a lot of energy. It frequently involves being cut off from loved ones who are there for you. For example, students who are away at university for the first time may perceive a lack of social support as a result of difficulties in forming new relationships.

Difficulties at home young people frequently report that school is where they feel most alone, whereas home is a calming environment. But feelings of loneliness can be exacerbated by difficulties at home, such as disagreements or tension with family members, the departure of supportive family members, or issues with mental health or substance abuse in the family. When lonely people try to talk about it, they sometimes feel like their parents are dismissing them.

Patterns of thinking

Loneliness is based on hypervigilance to social threats. As a result, lonely people tend to be on the lookout for aspects of their social world that could cause them to be rejected by others. Lonely young people may begin to view their interactions with others in a more critical light. Lonely people often blame themselves for their feelings and for not being able to make the connections they want. Because they believe it won't work, that can make it hard for them to try to connect with other people. Lonely people are more likely than others to view any lack of social skills as a trait that cannot be changed rather than a behavior that can be changed. As a result, the term "those experiencing loneliness" is used in this guide to emphasize that it is a condition that can be overcome; We don't talk about a "lonely person," which implies something that can't be changed.

In this guide, we will share what we have learned about how to get through loneliness, which stems from our extensive research into the experience of young people experiencing it. Lily's research focuses on learning from young people about how they feel about loneliness and how to deal with it. Pamela has studied youth loneliness for 25 years, making her a long-time expert in the field. Although it can be difficult to overcome, loneliness can ultimately help us connect with the people whose presence makes us feel our best.

CHAPTER TWO

What To Do?

Because loneliness is a complex experience, it cannot always be explained by a single factor and may not be alleviated by a single remedy. It's possible that what works for one person won't work for another. Don't give up hope if you're feeling lonely and nothing seems to be helping. Likely, you haven't found the approach that works best for you yet. Starting with things you can do on your own and moving on to ways to connect with others, here are some practical steps you can try:

Reexamine negative thoughts

because it can keep us stuck in a cycle of loneliness: It keeps us feeling low and prevents us from connecting with other people. Recognizing that just having a thought does not make it true can be helpful. For instance, you might think that your friend doesn't want to talk to you, but that doesn't mean it's true. Perhaps your friend is distracted by a problem. If we believe that our friends don't want to talk to us, it can make us feel further apart from them, encourage us to withdraw, and reinforce the impression that we are disconnected from them.

We can reevaluate the situation by drawing inspiration from cognitive behavioral therapy (CBT). Consider the scenario in which you speak to a group of friends and make a statement to which no one responds. Your typical response might be to accept the thought as true and remain silent if you then have the realization that no one is interested in what I have to say and that I should just keep quiet. Instead, you can question the thought's value to challenge it: Has it helped you to believe that "no one is interested"? Do you feel more or less acknowledged by your friends because you believe you should keep your mouth shut? Is there a different reason why no one responded? Instead of accepting negative thoughts as absolute truths, this might inspire you to consider other points of view.

Take the Initiative of deriving joy in alone time

Taking advantage of the advantages of spending time alone with enjoyable activities, such as going for a walk, reading, listening to music, or picking up a new hobby, can provide us with self-fulfillment while simultaneously removing us from our feelings. Instead of dwelling on negative thoughts and prolonging or intensifying those feelings, you are better able to let the emotions pass when you are alone by taking your mind off of how you are feeling.

There are additional advantages to alone time. It can provide you with the space to recharge and reflect on your life's events, especially when you spend a lot of time with others at school or work. Young people say they use the time alone as a chance to unwind or relax when they're frustrated.

Get creative with your lonely moment

Write about how you feel if you are currently uncomfortable discussing your feelings of loneliness with another person. That could be in a daily journal or a "brain dump" in which you record your thoughts as they come to you. You can learn more about the things that make you feel bad by writing them down. It's possible that you can figure out the pattern that your harrowing thoughts usually follow. You might, for instance, have an upsetting thought about an awkward interaction at school among the random thoughts that you don't pay much attention to: Do you recall my attempt to converse with Tom in class? It felt awkward. And you may notice that your response is to think even more unfavorable things about yourself: He was so blunt that it was obvious that he didn't want to talk to me, but I kept talking. I bet I seem so annoyed. Why do I act like that? No one wants to talk to me... The thought re-evaluation strategies described above can be started by writing down the thoughts that lead to more negative thinking.

Alternatively, you might find that making a piece of art that shows how you feel, like a drawing, a poem, or a song, helps you understand what's going on in your head. It might be helpful to start by writing or drawing how you feel if you don't feel like speaking up or if you don't have the words to tell someone how you feel. You can use what you create as a starting point for the conversation if you get to the point where you feel comfortable opening up.

Reach out to friends, counselors, and people who care and know about loneliness

If you are encountering dejection, you could find it overwhelming to converse with somebody about it. Maybe you dread that the individual you trust will be troubled by everything you say to them. Yet, by connecting, you could find that the individual you converse with has encountered something almost identical. Getting sympathetic and tolerating reactions from others about our concerns can assist with easing self-question, and thus improve our relationship with the individual we trust in. Consider whom you would feel generally open to opening up to, whether that is somebody you live with, like a parent, kin, or another relative, or somebody beyond your home, like a companion at school or in your area.

It could assist with beginning by framing why you are opening up, and what you wish to get from the discussion -, for example, whether you need their recommendation, or simply a listening ear. That way you lessen the probability of the individual answering such that you see it as pointless. One more method for starting is by discussing depression all the more, by and large, inquiring as to whether they have any insight of feeling desolate or have much familiarity with dejection. Furthermore, beginning with an up close and personal discussion isn't the main choice - you may be more open to opening up by talking over text or thinking of them in a letter.

If you want to converse with somebody, you know wouldn't be great for you, it could assist with conversing with a guide or clinician all things considered. At times, conversing with a not straightforwardly associated with your individual life and has no connections to individuals in it can have a good sense of reassurance. Moreover, an expert can guarantee that, in opening up, you stay zeroed in on tracking down arrangements rather than ruminating about adverse occasions. Addressing your primary care physician about finding a reasonable clinician is an effective method for the beginning. For understudies, school or college instructors are another expected asset. If you don't have up close and personal admittance to an expert, you could find a web-based directing help, for example, Childline in the Unified Realm, Emergency Text Line in the US, or Lifesaver in Australia.

Fix Plans

It is not always necessary to open up when reaching out. Perhaps you have been anticipating an invitation to socialize with classmates at your school. Instead, it might be beneficial to initiate contact first; You could keep things straightforward by scheduling a park or coffee walk. Naturally, you may be thinking: However, what if they decline? That is a risk, but you also avoid a potential connection by avoiding rejection.

Joining a group that focuses on a hobby or activity you enjoy, such as reading and discussing books or playing football, is another social initiative. Finding a club that focuses on your interests ensures that you and other members share at least one common interest; It indicates that you have something to talk about and have the potential to establish friendships with people who share your interests.

Increasing your community involvement can help you feel like you belong. Working together toward a common objective can be a great way to get involved and naturally form friendships through volunteering. Opportunities to volunteer can often be found by searching "volunteering in [your city]."Opportunities are likely to be advertised in your town's Facebook group.

Meet people online

Recognizing that not everyone has people with whom they can connect at their school is important. It's possible that you won't meet people at your school who share your interests and thoughts. You can find people who share your interests by joining an online group. Facebook groups are available for topics ranging from animal rights to your favorite band. If you want to meet people face to face, look for those in your area (for example, "K-pop fans London"). If you do decide to meet in person, just ensure that you do not disclose any personal information and that you do so in a public location and a group rather than one-on-one.) Although it is commonly believed that social media hurts young people, when used to directly communicate with friends, it can assist in the development of relationships and help alleviate feelings of isolation. You can also anonymously share your thoughts and feelings with others who have been through something similar in online forums.

Stop comparison with others

To stop comparing ourselves to other people is very difficult. We all do it, but just being aware that things are not always as they appear from the outside can be helpful.

On social media, for instance, we frequently only see what other people want to share about their lives, which can make us feel as though we are the only ones who are feeling lonely.

It is essential to keep in mind that you have no idea how other people feel when they are by themselves or when their social media feeds are disabled.

Additionally, research on self-esteem may assist you if you believe that your feelings of loneliness are exacerbated by a lack of confidence in yourself or your life compared to others.

Take it slow

Even if you already know a lot of people, trying to meet new people or opening up to them for the first time can be terrifying if you've been feeling lonely for a while. However, you are not required to act immediately.

You could try participating in online activities like a drawing lesson where you are not expected to interact with other people. Or, if you want to join a new group or class, you could ask the person in charge of the sessions if you can just watch at first instead of participating.

Some feelings of loneliness may be alleviated by the mere fact that others are present.

How to be less Lonely

While policymakers struggle to address loneliness as a social problem, there are individual actions we can take to alleviate loneliness. To help you feel less alone in this icy world, here are a few suggestions that are supported by evidence.

According to research, pursuing social groups rather than one-on-one interactions is much more effective at addressing feelings of loneliness.

For instance, researchers have discovered that group discussions outperform one-on-one visits to lonely elderly people.

This is significant because most of us typically attempt to combat loneliness by interacting with others. We believe that our lack of one-on-one interactions is the problem, even though group affiliations appear to be more to blame for loneliness.

What is the simplest way to join a group? Find something to do. The better the group, the more active and active it is.

Classes like dancing, swimming, gymnastics, and so on were discovered by research. decreased loneliness more than in classes in which everyone sat around and talked about random topics.

So, find a crowd. Find something to do.

They are other great ideas to overcome the state of loneliness and research has proven that this method is adopted and provides a highly significant phase to becoming a better version of what you are.

Other ideas to overcome loneliness

a. **Don't over- or under-prioritize.**

It's never good for you to give too much importance to someone or something, and the same goes for not giving enough importance to things that are important to your life.

Try not to cling too tightly to anything. When it comes to maintaining your inner self-sufficiency, it may not be your best friend to form firm beliefs about someone or something. It will greatly benefit you if you can begin to take life a little more lightly.

Even the most brutal discussions and serious debates that we all engage in from time to time and that have no direct connection to our lives will become fun banter for you and you will feel livelier and more energetic when you give only as much importance as is necessary. Decluttering your inner world and allowing it to flourish peacefully is probably one of the best things you can do, which indirectly helps you get over loneliness.

When you take a stand in favor of something, you are already opposed to something else as well. Additionally, that can occasionally result in internal conflict. You don't have to be against anyone who doesn't like red just because you like red more in a rainbow.

You can substitute the rainbow illustration for one hundred and twelve other instances in which you accord something more important than its merits. Your life will be much more peaceful and calming as a result.

b. "Everything is Right and Everything is Wrong"

If you start living your life with this mindset, you'll have fewer small fights and irrelevant arguments, and you'll feel more at ease with yourself than you did when you held on to certain ideas or beliefs.

This will give you a sense of freedom that is well worth experiencing. Additionally, this is a belief, which is amusing. A belief in and of itself is having no beliefs. A belief in no ideology is an ideology in and of itself.

The difference is that this type of belief will free you, while the others will enslave you. Most of the time, all it takes is a slight shift in perspective to turn even the most serious and serious of situations into something fun and easy.

And since we discussed that the main enemy is not loneliness but the constant flux of useless and power-sucking thoughts, anything that helps you sort out your inner world will help you overcome the fear of loneliness.

A Real-World Example (Breakup)

Let's say you and your partner broke up and are now all alone and depressed. As a result, there is a common perspective. Sing sad songs, get drunk, feel hopeless, and believe that life has no purpose, all while filling your head with negative thoughts.

The alternative might be to take it lightly and alter the situation's entire narrative. You can look at it this way: there were good and bad times when you started a relationship. The bad outweighed the good, which must have led to the breakup in the first place. If that's the case, aren't you supposed to be glad it happened? I mean, if that's what was going on in your relationship, shouldn't it be obvious that it's over now? You wouldn't have parted ways in the first place if everything had run smoothly and smoothly. But that's not how we see it. Your negative-biased brain would always keep reminding you of the good times you won't get to experience instead of the bad ones.

c. **stop clinging to the past.**

If you don't keep your memories, it can help you get over your loneliness a lot.

You won't have to dwell on your past any longer because you will be fully alive and aware of the present, which has so much to offer that you won't feel lonely. When you hold on to a few good memories, you become lonely, and your attachment to them is what makes you more lonely.

But if you raise your awareness and pay complete attention to what's going on around you, you'll realize that you don't need any memories to make this moment special. It is already novel and fresh. This moment was only made stale by your out-of-date thinking.

The Long-Term Solution to Loneliness

If I had to sum up this article, I would say that you can get over loneliness by following the tried-and-true advice that is all over the internet. They are unquestionably effective on a short-term basis and have the potential to provide you with a much-needed boost for some time.

However, realizing and accepting who you are is the only long-term solution to loneliness. This implies diving headfirst into the spiritual abyss and accepting without reservation that you are your happiness. You are the entire universe within yourself, not just a speck in space.

The only reason you feel sad or alone is that you have been misinterpreting who you are. To comprehend the depths of reality, one needs to have a very still and peaceful mind.

Although I am aware that all of this must sound rather foolish, impractical, and naive, I assure you that this is the entire solution. You can start digging in on your own, so you don't have to rely on me. It is your responsibility to provide you with a small glimmer of hope at the end of a dark tunnel; my job is done. You have two options: you can look, find out, and reach the moon, or you can dismiss it as nothing more than a mirage.

Let's get it. I have also been there, as have you. This feeling of being alone, as if the world and you are separate entities, secluded from everyone, must have affected at least a couple of billion people at some point in their lives. As if nobody will rescue you from the cliff you are falling from or from the upside-down car that is about to explode and kill you.

It truly stinks. The whole experience becomes even more agonizing and soul-sucking because we suck even more at knowing how to overcome loneliness. You can be Superman on the outside as much as you want, but most people on the inside are terrified of being alone.

Physical and mental loneliness can go hand in hand. Physically, when no one wants to be with you and you always feel like you're by yourself. Mental: Even though you are constantly surrounded by people, you don't feel safe or connected to them on a mental level, and you always feel like there is a lack or a void that needs to be filled. Naturally, overcoming mental loneliness is harder than physical loneliness.

We are apprehensive at the mere thought of becoming alone, and we are hesitant to part ways with our friends and family. Although it is more terrifying than being alone, this is kind of a prelude to it.

If you had to choose between being already alone or constantly living in constant fear of becoming alone one day if, oh my God, the people closest to you were no longer around, you probably would choose the former, but that isn't good enough. We should all be skilled at overcoming loneliness.

CHAPTER THREE

Dark Side of Loneliness

However, this does not address the reason why I believe loneliness to be the hidden cause of so many contemporary social and cultural issues.

Social animals are what we are biological. We are designed to live in groups and physically rely on one another. As a result, our emotional dependence on one another has evolved as well.

Our relationships with other people or our perception of our place in society as a whole account for a significant portion of our sense of purpose and meaning in life. It would appear that our need for human connection is so strong that our relationships are largely responsible for our capacity to form practical beliefs about ourselves and the world. If you don't use your empathy, you lose it, just like a muscle.

Therefore, when people investigate the underlying loneliness that drives political extremists, conspiracy theorists, and religious fanatics, they consistently discover this. People become radicalized by rejection and social isolation. People, in search of a sense of purpose, resort to delusional notions of revolution and world preservation in the absence of affection and understanding.

Hannah Arendt, a German Jew who escaped the Nazis with success, was a philosopher and writer who lived in the middle of the 20th century. She studied totalitarianism, the rise and fall of fascism, communist revolutions, the horrors of Stalin, Hitler, Mussolini, and Mao, and, more importantly, why these leaders became so popular among their followers so quickly despite the terror they invoked. She did this for years after the war.

After that, she published The Origins of Totalitarianism, a classic work. She comes to a shocking conclusion at the end of the nearly 500-page book: She argued that being alone makes people susceptible to the disdain and division that lead to extremism and violence in functioning societies.

I'll quote her extensively here, and I hope her children won't sue me:

"Loneliness, the common ground for terror, the essence of totalitarian government, the preparation of its executioners and victims, is closely associated with uprootedness and meaninglessness, which have been the curse of modern masses since the beginning of the industrial revolution and became acute with the rise of imperialism at the end of the last century and the breakdown of political institutions and social traditions in our own time.

The fact that loneliness, once a borderline experience typically experienced in certain marginal social conditions like old age, has become an everyday experience of the ever-growing masses of our century is what prepares men for totalitarian dominance in the non-totalitarian world. Totalitarianism's brutal process of driving and organizing the masses seems like a suicide attempt to escape this reality. In a world where nobody is trustworthy and nothing can be relied upon, the reasoning that "seizes you as in a vise" appears to be a last resort. The strict avoidance of contradiction that appears to confirm a man's identity outside of relationships is the only content of inner coercion. “12 In essence, once we are cut off from social contact that helps us feel grounded, the only way we can understand the world is by adopting radical all-or-nothing views. People also begin to recognize the necessity of a radical change in the status quo within these perspectives. They begin to envision themselves as either destined saviors of society or complete victims.

Also, keep in mind that she wrote this in 1951, long before it was thought that Trump, woke leftists, and Twitter had ruined everything.

And this may be the real threat posed by social media: It simply makes it possible for the lonely, enraged, selfish, and spiteful to self-organize and be heard like never before—it does not necessarily make us lonelier, angrier, more selfish, or more spiteful.

In the past, you kind of had to keep that nonsense to yourself if you were a radical Marxist who wanted a violent revolution or a liar who thought Bill Gates was implanting microchips in millions of African children. Until you realized you weren't being invited to kids' birthday parties anymore, you'd cause a lot of awkward silences and shifty side glances.

Therefore, you ought to shut up. And eventually, you would begin to realize that the majority of people are fine. Everything will be fine.

Now, then? Somewhere, there is a forum full of people who feel exactly like you do. And when a group of people with similar but strange beliefs get together, what do they do? That's right; they convince themselves that their knowledge will save the world. That is, they embark on a mission. They have to explain to us at Thanksgiving why Jesus was a communist, why the movie Armageddon was a coded message from a certain source, and why Bruce Willis doesn't just run a pedophile ring; rather, he is secretly a sixteen-year-old boy being held prisoner against his wishes. You, I, and everyone else has to listen to them because they are encouraged and inspired by their new internet "friends."

Regardless, where was I?

Yes, yes! Loneliness. Perhaps a different perspective on Arendt's argument is that we run the risk of extremists taking control if it becomes easier for radicals with fringe beliefs to mobilize and organize than for the majority of more moderate people. Historically, economic depressions, famines, pandemics, and other similar events enabled this mobilization of the extremes. Perhaps smartphones and social media have unintentionally made it easier to mobilize people today.

However, who knows? I might be wrong about everything. The fact of the matter is that we do not yet know enough to be sure.

Loneliness haunts many people, particularly codependents.60 million Americans, or 20 percent, say that their suffering stems from loneliness. According to Cacioppo and Patrick (2008), the brain region known as the dorsal anterior cingulate is where we get our emotional response to rejection.

Contrasting Loneliness with Aloneness Loneliness is associated with living alone, which, according to surveys, has steadily increased to 27% in 2013 and 50% or higher in particular parts of California, West Virginia, and Florida.

However, being alone and alone only refers to a physical state. When we are by ourselves, we don't always feel lonely. Different people have different needs for connection. Some people choose to live on their own and find that it makes them happier. They do not experience the same sense of abandonment that is brought on by the unwelcome death, divorce, or breakup of a partner. Recent research suggests that they may also inherit a greater insensitivity to social isolation.

Loneliness in Relationships Although individuals who live on their own are more likely to experience loneliness, it can also be felt in a relationship or group. This is because the quality of our social interactions, not the quantity, is what makes us feel connected. Family dinners have decreased as the number of work hours and televisions in the home has increased. Even though there are more interactions now, screen time is taking the place of face time as a result of the proliferation of cell phones. According to Cacioppo (2012), people spend more time online than they do in person, which makes them feel more alone.

According to a UCLA study, this is causing a decline in social skills. New technology is making college students less empathetic by 40%, and 12-year-olds are acting socially like 8-year-olds. According to a recent survey conducted by Pew Research Center, 82% of adults believed that their use of smartphones in social settings harmed conversation.

Lack of intimacy and codependency When we don't have someone to listen to us, care about us, and affirm our existence, we feel alone or emotionally abandoned. Even though close relationships are the solution, codependent relationships typically lack intimacy. Shame and lack of communication make intimacy difficult for codependents. They frequently have a partner who is addicted, abusive, or just emotionally unavailable (though they may also be).

Codependents may be unable to pinpoint the cause of their unhappiness, whether they are living on their own or in a relationship. They might not be aware that they are alone, but they might be depressed, sad, or bored. Others are aware, but they struggle to effectively solicit their requirements. The emotional dysfunction they experienced as children, their relationship dynamics, and their feelings of isolation, may appear comparable. We long for and require emotional closeness from our friends and partners, but when there isn't a strong emotional connection, we feel disconnected and empty.

I didn't realize it was something less tangible, real intimacy, that was lacking in my relationship when I believed years ago that more shared activities would create that missing connection. Check out "Your Intimacy

Index.")Instead, like the majority of codependent people, I experienced "pseudo-intimacy," which can be a romantic "fantasy bond," shared activities, intense sexuality, or a relationship in which only one partner is vulnerable while the other serves as an advisor, confidant, provider, or emotional caretaker.

Childhood loneliness and a persistent lack of connection are the root causes of the undercurrent of loneliness and fear of loneliness. While some children are abused or neglected, the majority of them grow up in homes where their parents lack the time or emotional resources to care for their feelings and needs. Children experience feelings of rejection, shame, and isolation. Even though their family appears to be normal, some people feel like they are an outsider and that "No one understands me." They withdraw, conform, rebel, or engage in addictions as a means of coping, masking and eventually denying their inner feelings.

Loneliness and Shame In the meantime, a growing sense of separation from oneself and a lack of genuine connection with one or more parents can lead to feelings of inner loneliness and unworthiness. Shame stems from the awareness of human separation without love-based reunion. It is simultaneously the cause of guilt and anxiety. Fromm, E., The Art of Loving, page 9) Codependents can become trapped in a vicious cycle of loneliness, shame, and depression as adults. A vicious cycle of abandonment can be exacerbated by relationship breakups and multiple breakups.

The lonelier we are, the less we want to interact with other people and the more anxious we become about making an authentic connection. Long-term loneliness is associated with low self-esteem, introversion, pessimism, disagreeableness, rage, shyness, anxiety, diminished social skills, and neuroticism, according to studies. Shame anxiety is when we imagine that other people will judge us poorly. This results in negative, anxious, and self-protective behaviors, which are met with negative responses from others, achieving our imagined outcome.

Loneliness hurts more than just ourselves. Because loneliness is stigmatized, we avoid speaking up about it. It is also experienced by people of different genders. Even though more women than men report feeling lonely, men who are alone are viewed in a negative light by women and men alike (Lau, 1992).

Health risks It is well known that loneliness and depression are strongly linked. Our endocrine, immune, and cardiovascular systems are all negatively impacted by loneliness, which also has a fatally accelerating effect on our health. A recent study found that lonely people are more likely to get cancer, neurodegenerative diseases, and viral infections.

The stress response of flight or fight is triggered by perceived loneliness. Exercise and quality restful sleep is reduced while stressing hormones and inflammation increase. Norepinephrine surges, increasing the production of white blood cells that cause inflammation and shutting down immune functions. In the meantime, it makes us less sensitive to the inflammation-fighting hormone cortisol.

Turhan Canli, a neuroscientist, makes the following observation in response to the research: "The self-reinforcing, negative, emotional spiral that was discussed earlier is confirmed by the fact that loneliness affects our genetic inflammatory response the following year." According to Chen (2015), "loneliness predicted changes in biology, and changes in biology predicted changes in loneliness."

Coping with Being Alone Sometimes, even though it would be helpful, we may not want to talk to anyone. We now have the evidence to explain why biological and even genetic changes make it difficult to overcome loneliness. Many of us tend to isolate even more when we are alone. Instead of trying to connect with others, we might engage in addictive behavior. Obesity is strongly associated with feelings of loneliness.

We must fight our instinct to withdraw. Try telling a neighbor or friend that you're lonely. Commit to attending a 12-step meeting, a class, a meetup, CoDA, or another one to encourage socializing with other people. Exercise with someone else. Volunteering or supporting a friend in need can help you relax and feel better.

Loneliness is exacerbated by resistance and self-criticism, as it is with all emotions. If we allow our hearts to open, we worry that we will suffer even more. Frequently, the opposite is true. The energy spent suppressing feelings can also be released by allowing them to flow. We experience a shift in our emotional state, resulting in feelings of vigor, tranquility, exhaustion, or contentment when we are alone.

What we don't know about Loneliness

Okay, that certainly sounds awful. But wait, there's more: there are still a lot of things we don't know about loneliness:

Why this is taking place? The western world appears to suffer from loneliness more than other cultures. There are numerous explanations for this, but we still lack solid answers. Westerners have a more individualistic culture that places less emphasis on family or community, according to some. Some attribute the problem to urbanization and cultural norms regarding living alone, working independently, and owning one's own home. Some point to shifts in the population: People are moving around more frequently, having fewer children, and spending less time with the elderly. Even though religion has historically been the foundation of human community and camaraderie, some point to the decline in religiosity. Any or all of these could be the case.

how to correct it Again, there are numerous hypotheses, but very little is known for sure. Online and mobile connections appear to be inadequate substitutes for the social and emotional nourishment we receive from others. Video games and social media are like the diet soda of our emotional health—they taste like we're having fun, but they don't give us any emotional energy. Furthermore, we are starved if we do not consume emotional calories in this instance. The quantity and quality of social interactions affect loneliness. Not only do we need to see people we know often, but we also need to be able to trust and feel close to them.

However, attempts are being made. The UK appointed a "minister of loneliness" in 2018." Co-housing policies," which "match" elderly, retired, and young families in need of childcare into housing units where they share living spaces and support each other, are working well in Scandinavian nations like Denmark. However, this appears to be a significant issue overall. This is a problem to the point where the medical community has noticed, and pharmaceutical companies are even wondering if they could come up with a medication to treat loneliness in the same way that depression pills do.

What is the Deal with Loneliness

The western world is rife with loneliness. Sociologists have discovered that 10-15% of Americans will most likely die alone, and that number will continue to rise in the coming decades.

According to numerous surveys conducted in the United States and Europe, anywhere from 30 to 60 percent of the population self-reports experiencing feelings of loneliness and or stating that they do not engage in meaningful in-person interactions daily.

The fact that younger people frequently report feeling more lonely than older people is even more surprising.

Let's just make it known. Being alone is unhealthy. Loneliness has been linked to shorter lifespans as much as smoking 15 cigarettes per day, according to a well-known statistic.

However absurd their method of calculating these factoids is, the point remains: Physically and mentally, loneliness is unhealthy. Anxiety and depression are increased as a result.

Additionally, it affects your physical health. Loneliness increases the risk of heart disease, high blood pressure, and weakened immune systems, according to studies.

Conclusion

Being in love itself is the ultimate goal or means of overcoming loneliness. Give rather than seek.

If you can be like this, you'll feel just as great when you're by yourself as when you're in a group. The incessant stream of "not so amazing" thoughts that consume people is the single most important factor in their inability to feel this way.

What if, on the other hand, your thoughts become your best friends? What if your thoughts are the only thing keeping you entertained all the time? The issue was resolved then. The feeling of being alone won't be able to get the better of you if you can fully enjoy your own company.

And unlike everyone else, you won't try to connect with people or things outside of yourself just to keep yourself happy. Instead, when you're living your own business to the fullest, you won't need to connect with anyone else because everyone wants to connect with someone like you. Therefore, when the root of the issue is within you, put an end to accumulating things on the outside. Outside, you don't have any control, but inside, you can. You can't just ignore the negative aspects of any object or person you come into contact with on the outside and just enjoy the positive aspects for the rest of your life.

And because you don't have this control, you won't ever be truly content and happy inside. In this world, nothing is white or black; they are both the same. Therefore, your futile attempt to swallow the white and throw away the black will fail. As a result, it's wise to realize that you are complete and whole on your own and that you don't need anyone else to make you happy.

www.ingramcontent.com/pod-product-compliance
Lightning Source LLC
LaVergne TN
LVHW052107160826
845678LV00015B/3407

9798356127175